NATIONAL GEOGRAPHIC

School Publishing

Recycling Rules!

PATHFINDER EDITION

By Barbara Keeler

CONTENTS

Recycling Rules!

By Barbara Keeler

In the U.S., the average family of four throws out 2,907 kilograms (6,409 pounds) of paper, glass, plastic, food scraps, and other trash each year. That's about as much as 115 third graders weigh! Those pounds of trash add up. It can pollute the planet and hurt wildlife.

The good news is that people can recycle some of this trash. You've probably dropped containers into a recycle bin. What happens after that? A truck hauls them to a recycling plant. There, the solid containers are melted into liquids. Then the liquids are made into new solids. People can then use the new solids. Using solids again means less trash for the Earth.

Recycling Resources

W hy is recycling important? People are quickly using up Earth's resources to make new things. But when people recycle, Earth is not harmed to get new resources. Recycling also saves energy because making new products uses a lot of energy.

Trashing the Earth

Trash is made up of solids, liquids, and gases. A lot of trash ends up in a **landfill.** Solids have a definite shape, but liquids and gases take the shape of their containers. All these kinds of matter take up space.

That means landfills can take up a lot of room. Think about a half-empty juice can. The solid metal takes up space whether or not it's flattened. Any leftover juice, or liquid, in the can also takes up space. Even the air in the can, which is a gas, takes up space.

Trash Heap. Some cities run out of space for landfills. Recycling helps to keep some items out of landfills.

Stripped Bare. Miners have stripped this forest land to mine **bauxite** ore. This is used to make aluminum products.

Recycling Glass

Glass is an item that is often recycled. Glass containers are sorted by color. Next, the glass is crushed and melted in a furnace.

Molten glass pours out of the furnace. The molten glass is blown into molds. It cools, hardens back into a solid, and is taken out of the mold. Then it is cut into pieces to make a bottle or a jar.

Recycling one glass jar saves enough energy to light a 100-watt lightbulb for four hours.

Recycling Metals

Have you ever recycled a can? What happens to it? First, it goes to a recycling plant. There, giant blades shred it up. Next, the coatings are removed. Then a huge furnace changes it from solid to liquid. Melting an old can into liquid metal doesn't use nearly as much energy as it takes to make new liquid metal.

The molten, or melted, metal may be formed into bars and cooled into solids. Later, the bars are squeezed flat between huge rollers. Then they are rolled into sheets of metal to make new cans.

Recycling Plastic

Plastic can last for hundreds of years. So we might as well reuse it! Some plastics are melted and recycled much like glass. Recycled plastic gets used for a lot of things. You probably walk on recycled plastic every day. Some carpet fiber is made using it. You probably also wear recycled plastic. Polyester clothing is often made from it.

Plastic is harder to recycle than glass. Why? Not all plastic is the same. Each type contains different materials with different properties. Some plastics melt at different temperatures than others. That makes it hard for recycling plants to recycle them.

A lot of trash changes from solids to liquids and back to solids during the recycling process. Solids can be melted and formed into new products. Sometimes gases are added. Adding gas into some kinds of liquid plastic makes plastic foam for insulated cups.

We can recycle a lot of trash by changing its state.

Tree Musketeers

The city of El Segundo, California, picks up and recycles plastic. Brook Church remembers when El Segundo had no recycling program. That's why he started one at age 12. He, his ten-year-old sister, and some friends were in a group called Tree Musketeers.

Making a Difference. Tree Musketeers helped residents recycle until the city set up a program. By 2009, Tree Musketeers had won four Presidential awards.

Tree Musketeers began by writing columns about recycling in the newspaper. Then they set up some huge bins. People dropped off recyclables. Parents drove the solids to a recycling center.

After a few years, people in El Segundo wanted their recycling to be picked up from their homes. This is called curbside pickup. Tree Musketeers asked the city council to start picking up **recyclables** at the curb. The council said no. So Tree Musketeers found another way.

Success!

Tree Musketeers called a waste hauler. The waste hauler agreed to pick up recyclables for a fee. The program cost people $6.00 a month. Tree Musketeers collected payments to pay for the waste hauler.

Finally, after 13 years, the city took over. The city started picking up recyclables from every home. Curbside pickup was free.

Recycling Everywhere

Now many cities have curbside recycling. Kids all over the country are making recycling a part of their lives.

The kids in Santa Rosa Beach, Florida, helped to make it easier to recycle in their community. The kids worked to get more blue bags for the blue bag program. With this program, people put their recyclables into blue bags. The bags are picked up with the rest of the trash. At the landfill, workers separate the blue bags from the rest of the trash. Then the recyclables are taken to recycling plants! Some places do the same thing, just with different color bags.

Gwen Wright's 1st-grade class at Butler Elementary in Florida led the way. The class collected 239 student signatures for a petition. The petition asked stores to sell blue bags. Some stores began to sell them. As the bags became popular, the county gave out some free bags.

It takes energy to melt solids for recycling. In Santa Rosa Beach, Florida, **Ella Robinson is learning not to make solid trash in the first place.** Ella takes her own cloth napkin and washes her own dishes at school. When Ella shops with her grandmother, they take their own shopping bags.

These kids and many others are working hard to make recycling a bigger part of their communities.

Watching Your Waste: **The 4 Rs**

Here are a few ways you can help reduce waste.

REDUCE

Buy things with no or little packaging.
Take your own bags to the store.
Take your own cups when you buy drinks.
Buy reusable, not disposable (dishes, napkins, towels, dishcloths).
Compost, or make into fertilizer, yard waste and some food scraps.

REUSE

Reuse containers (boxes, bags, bottles, jars, plastic tubs).
Write notes on used paper.
Buy used things. Repair, sell, or give away old things.

RECYCLE

Look for recycling bins when you are out.
Write to companies that make plastic containers. Ask them to
   put symbols on lids so recycling centers will take them.

RECLAIM

Buy products made from recycled materials.
Buy products with recycled packaging and containers.

Wordwise

bauxite: the ore from which aluminum is made

landfill: an area of land where trash is stored

recyclables: things that can be made into new products

Clunkers
From the Road to the Recycler

As cars get old, sometimes they are no longer good for driving. People sometimes call these cars clunkers. Some of them are sold for scrap. Many of their parts are recycled.

The car parts shown here can be reused on other cars.

windows

windshield

front end

back end

wheel

body panels

What happens when a clunker is sold for scrap? First, the liquids, such as oil, are removed. Some are recycled. Then some of the parts of the car are sold and reused.

Next, the car is often flattened and crushed. The parts are shredded. Huge magnets separate the metals from the rest of the matter. Then the metals are melted down and formed into other products.

What happens to the tires? Many landfills will not accept tires. They take up too much space and don't break down very easily. Good tires are used on other cars. Some are used for other purposes, such as building walls to stop flooding. Others are recycled without being melted. They may be cut up and used for other products, such as sandals. Some tires are ground and shredded. They are used in carpet padding or as filler for roads.

Recycling Rules!

Recycling matters! Answer these questions to see what you've learned.

1 List three reasons to recycle.

2 How is metal recycled?

3 Why is plastic harder to recycle than metal?

4 How did Tree Musketeers change recycling in their community?

5 What are old tires used for after they are recycled?

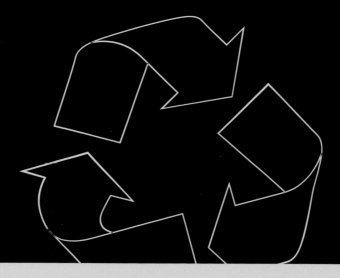